CHRIST JESUS

The Truth

Book II

Sister Mary Joan Agresta, S.N.D.
Sister Mary Renée Pastor, S.N.D.
Sister Mary Reiling, S.N.D.

Theological Advisor
Rev. John A. Hardon, S.J.

Consultants
Rev. Daniel L. Flaherty, S.J.
Rev. Fred Henley, S.J.
Rev. Daniel A. Murray
Rev. Msgr. Joseph T. Moriarty

General Editor
Sister Mary de Angelis Bothwell, S.N.D.

s to _____

D1501800

CHRIST OUR LIFE SE
LOYOLA UNIVERSITY PRESS, Chicago 60657

ISBN 8294-0412-0

NIHIL OBSTAT Reverend Robert Labella, M.S. TH.M.
Censor Deputatus

IMPRIMATUR Most Reverend Anthony M. Pilla, D.D. M.A.
Bishop of Cleveland

Given at Cleveland, Ohio, October 29, 1982

ACKNOWLEDGMENTS

The general editor and authors wish to thank Sister Mary Raphaelita, Sister Mary Christopher, Sister Mary Elizabeth, and Sister Mary Nathan who have made the revision of Christ Jesus possible. So many people have actually helped in the revision process that it is difficult to acknowledge them all. We would like to express our gratitude to all who have guided us, inspired us, prayed for us, offered suggestions, tried things out in classrooms, and critiqued the manuscript. The feedback from hundreds of catechists using the original edition has been invaluable.

We are proud to acknowledge the particular contributions of Sister Mary Theresa Betz, Sister Mary Andrew Miller and our deceased Sister Mary Patricia Lab. Particular acknowledgment and thanks are due to Sister Mary Jude Volzer and the other Sisters of Notre Dame who planned, organized, and wrote the original edition. Many catechists provided ideas which have been incorporated into the revision. We are especially grateful to Sisters Jane Marie Reisinger, Mary Margaret Kerr, Suzanne Marie Nelson, Mary Virginia Turner, Rita Marie Miklitsch, Mary Judith Ostrowski, Mary Tanya Klement and innumerable others for their contributions and to Sister Regina Marie Alfonso for checking the reading level of this book. We are especially grateful to Sister Mary Catherine Rennecker whose encouragement and countless hours of typing and retyping the manuscript helped make this book possible. It was a privilege to work with her.

Books are not simply written, they are produced by many people. We want to acknowledge Carol Tornatore, Deborah Astudillo, and Mary Hollowed at Loyola Press who transformed our manuscript into the attractive manual and perform-a-text. Most of the photographs were taken by Michael Nabicht and Patrick Delahanty of Ikonographics, Inc., Louisville, Kentucky, with the joint cooperation of Reverend William F. Walsh, O.S.F.S., and the students from Bishop Ireton High School and Sister Alice Condon, C.S.C., and the students from St. Mary's Academy in Alexandria, Virginia; Sister Mary Dolores Vargo and the students of St. John School in McLean, Virginia; Sister Mary Antoinette Krejsa and the students from Our Lady of Victory School in Washington, D.C.; Sister Mary Julianna Novey and the students and families of St. Agnes Parish in Arlington, Virginia. Photographs on the pages indicated were taken by Gloria Denos: 1, 9, 12, 29, 49, 51. George Lane, S.J.: 2, 37. Mark Link, S.J.: 5, 45. A special thank you to Jack Noble White and St. Anthony Messenger Press for the use of material from Everything You Need for Children's Worship* (*Except Children).

This revision follows the guidelines of Pope John Paul II's Apostolic Exhortation "On Catechesis in Our Times" and Sharing the Light of Faith: National Catechetical Directory for Catholics of the United States. It implements the recommendations in the Rite of Christian Initiation of Adults, Moral Education and Christian Conscience and Respect Life Curriculum Guidelines produced by the Department of Education, United States Catholic Conference.

Excerpts from The Jerusalem Bible, 1966 by Darton, Longman and Todd, Ltd. and Doubleday & Company, Inc. used by permission of the publisher. Excerpt from the English translation of The Roman Missal, 1973 by International Committee on English in the Liturgy, Inc. (ICEL).

Cover photo: Arizona Highways
Illustrated by Mary Hollowed
Design by Carol Tornatore

TABLE OF CONTENTS

NOTE TO STUDENTS

One of the most important decisions you can make in life is the decision to dedicate your life to Jesus and His kingdom. That is to dedicate yourself to a life of knowing and living the truth. Jesus said: "I am the Truth." Because He is the Truth He is also the perfect witness to the Truth. You can rely on His words and His example as you can rely on no other.

Jesus teaches us the true way to live—a way that is different from any other in the world. He gives us not only a new law to follow but Himself, Who is the Truth.

CHRIST JESUS, THE TRUTH is the second in a series of three books written to help you know Jesus, to commit yourself to Him through your daily decisions, and to grow in a deeper friendship with Him. When you use this book you will discover what Jesus taught and how to form your values according to His.

Jesus was the happiest man who ever lived. He knew what life was all about and He lived it to the full. He was also the most successful man who ever lived. Though seemingly His life was a failure (crucifixion as a criminal), it accomplished what no other life could accomplish: the redemption and salvation of the entire human family. Only He can communicate to you the meaning of your life and show you how to make it a success—an eternal success.

Jesus, through His Spirit of Truth within you, will help you in making day-to-day decisions. He will inspire you to love and to be of service to others in creative ways. When you make decisions according to His values, you will build the Christian community and make His kingdom alive to all around you.

This book will give you a deeper appreciation of the challenge of living Christ's new law of love. Reflect often on these words of St. Paul which describe the way Christ Jesus, The Truth, calls you to live.

> Out of His infinite glory, may He give you the power through His Spirit for your hidden self to grow strong so that Christ may live in your hearts through faith and then planted in love and built on love, you will with all the saints have the strength to grasp the breadth and the length, the height and the depth until knowing the love of Christ which is beyond all knowledge you are filled with the utter fulness of God. Glory be to Him whose power working in us can do infinitely more than we can ask or imagine.
>
> *Ephesians 3:16-20*

You were darkness once, but now you are light in the Lord; be like children of light, for the effects of light are seen in complete goodness and right living in truth.

Ephesians 5:8-9

A Light in the Darkness

Have you ever groped or stumbled along a path because it was dark and you could not see? What would have helped you see the obstacles in the way and skirt around them?

Jesus calls Himself the Light of the World. He urges us to follow Him because He is the source of all that is true. How secure and confident we are when we follow His way! No matter how dark things appear, His teachings can illumine our way to the Father. When we follow His teachings, Jesus will help us deal with our problems in a way that will lead us safely to His kingdom.

JESUS AS TEACHER

Jesus, true God and true man, revealed the glory and love of God. Everything Jesus said and did teaches us some truth about God and human life. Through Jesus, God Himself has given us knowledge of divine things. This knowledge allows us to find God. It allows us to experience the happiness of friendship with Jesus. Jesus, the Son of God made man, is the only totally reliable teacher. He proclaimed the message of salvation. He assured us that God is always with us to deliver us from all evil and to bring us to eternal life with Himself. Our faith then is founded on what God Himself has revealed, especially through Jesus, His Son.

WHERE THIS MESSAGE IS FOUND

Christ the Lord commissioned His apostles to preach the entire Gospel message. They faithfully handed it on, both by word and by example. As people began to live according to that teaching, religious customs developed. Prayers and professions of faith were formulated to express the truths handed down. The message of Jesus is found in both the Scriptures and Tradition.

The Scriptures are the inspired written Word of God. Through them we can know the truth God has revealed about Himself and His plan for all He has created. But not everything God has revealed is recorded in Scripture.

Sacred Tradition is another means by which we come to know what God has revealed. It is the message of Jesus which was handed on by the spoken words and example of the apostles and through the Catholic Church.

THE CHURCH AS TEACHER

Jesus gave the pope and the bishops the right and duty to teach everything He had revealed. That is why the Church teaches doctrines that are found not only in Scripture but also in Tradition. In fact, the Church was in existence for some years before any of the New Testament was written.

Truth does not change, but the Church grows in its understanding of the truth Jesus taught. The Church is always accurate in teaching the truth Jesus shared with us. This truth, whether found in Scripture or Tradition, should guide all the decisions made by the Church and its members.

When people are too concerned about their own needs, they can easily overlook some truths. They can even ignore the truth or turn away from it.

The Holy Spirit guides the Church to a deeper understanding of God's message as the human family matures. When new insights are proclaimed by the teaching authority of the Church, we know they are true. Through the centuries the Church has preserved the doctrine Jesus taught and has gained many insights into its full meaning.

DO YOU KNOW?

Use the glossary to understand the words introduced in this section. Write the proper word or phrase from the Word Box in the blank spaces provided below.

Word Box	
doctrine	Scripture
profession of faith	Tradition

formulation of truths believed_____

any truth taught by the Church for all the faithful as absolutely true_____

written source of truths about God and His plan_____

any truths of Jesus' message not recorded in the Scriptures_____

SHED LIGHT ON THE TRUTH

On the lines below explain each statement.

1 Our faith is founded on divine, not human, teachings.

_____

_____

2 Some of the teachings of the Church are not found in the Scriptures.

_____

_____

3 The Church grows in understanding of the meaning of Jesus' teachings.

_____

_____

TEACHING IN PARABLES

When Jesus taught, He talked about things that people were familiar with. He spoke about sowers and seeds, fishermen and nets, shepherds and wolves, flour and yeast. He talked about common experiences: a lost coin, a widow pleading with a judge, a servant going about his work, a friend asking for help. Jesus compared what He wanted to teach to something people already knew. The stories Jesus told about God and His kingdom are called *parables*. In each parable Jesus taught something about loving God and respecting oneself and others.

Jesus' stories were easy to understand. They were easy to remember, and they had a message. But the message was more than a maxim. The parables often called people to discover how their way of thinking, their way of doing things, was different from God's way.

The parables can bring us to understand Jesus and His mission. They can help us see that the kingdom of God is not like an earthly one. It is beyond this world but it begins in this world. It is a world where God and His people live together in peace and love forever. In God's kingdom, even on earth, every person is treated justly and enjoys the freedom that human dignity demands.

When we hear a parable, we make a judgment about the people in the story. Jesus tells us to take that judgment and apply it to our own life. Each parable calls us to accept the truth Jesus proclaims, to welcome Jesus' message as a light showing us the way to the Father. When we apply a parable to our own life, we discover that it gives us a new way of looking at things. We become inspired to change our way of judging things and to love others with God's love.

NAME THE PARABLE

Below are some of the truths Jesus taught in His parables. Match the name of the parable with the truth each one teaches. Write the letter of the truth on the blank. Use the Scriptures to help you.

PARABLE	TRUTH REVEALED
1 _____ The Pharisee and the Publican (Lk 18:9-14)	a No matter how you have sinned, God forgives you when you turn back to Him.
2 _____ The Lost Sheep (Lk 15:4-7)	b People who have spent most of their lives in sin can still be forgiven and be with God for all eternity.
3 _____ The Laborers in the Vineyard (M 20:1-16)	c God doesn't judge a person only by his or her words and actions; it's what is in the heart that counts.
4 _____ The Rich Fool (Lk 12:16-21)	d God gives His grace to all people, but not everyone accepts it.
5 _____ The Sower and the Seed (Mk 4:3-9)	e Money and possessions are dangerous. People who are not alert can become enslaved by them.

Parables about the Kingdom

All the parables in Chapter 13 of Matthew's Gospel are parables of the kingdom of heaven. The parables of the kingdom urge us to open our hearts to the riches of God. They point out that the growth of the kingdom of God is a mystery which calls us to trust that God's ways are better than ours.

In the parable of the sower (Matthew 13:4-9) we learn that some people do not understand God's kingdom. Some accept the kingdom at first but are too weak to remain in it. The actions of some slow up the growth of the kingdom, while the actions of others may seem to choke it. Yet no one can ever really succeed in stopping the growth of God's kingdom.

In another parable Jesus compares the kingdom of heaven to a treasure. A man who finds a treasure and recognizes its worth is happy to offer all his goods to get the treasure. And people who discover the value of living in the kingdom of God happily give up many pleasures and comforts because they have found greater joys.

Jesus also spoke about a man who set out in search of pearls. When he had found the most lovely and costly pearl he had ever seen, he gladly gave up everything else to purchase it.

Why do you think this man gave up other things for this pearl?

_____

_____

What do you know about the Church as the kingdom of God on earth? Write your answers in the space provided.

1   Jesus expects His Church to proclaim Him and His way to the world. But human failure and sin within the Church distort the image of Jesus.
    What does Matthew 13:24-30 teach us about this?

    _____

    _____

2   Jesus tells us that the kingdom of God is a priceless treasure. Sometimes people who seek riches, power, popularity, and pleasure learn that this is true. What may happen in their lives to teach them that nothing but Jesus can really satisfy them?

    _____

    _____

CAN YOU COMPLETE THESE ANALOGIES?

An *analogy* is a comparison of one thing with another that is like it in a certain way. Here is an example: "A hand is to a glove as a foot is to a shoe." The hand and foot are compared to one another in one way that they are alike: a protective covering is put on both. The analogy can be written like this: "A hand : a glove :: a foot : a shoe." It is read, "Hand is to glove as foot is to shoe." Now try to complete these analogies which involve the parables listed.

1   Matthew 13:31-32
    The mustard seed : the shrub :: Jesus' aspostles : _____

2   Matthew 13:33
    The leaven : dough :: missionaries : _____

3   Matthew 13:33
    The yeast : dough :: true followers of Jesus : _____

4   Matthew 13:31-32
    The mustard seed : shrub :: good Christian parents : _____

PARABLES OF CRISIS

A crisis is a turning point. After a crisis people are never the same as they were before. Sometimes a crisis brings a person to a firm and definite change for the good. But sometimes a person is unwilling to face the crisis and becomes bitter instead.

Some of the parables of the kingdom are called crisis parables. In those stories Jesus contrasts the way different people behave in a similar situation. The crisis parables warn us not to postpone doing things until it is too late. They help us think about what we should do while we still have time.

Read Matthew 25:1-13 and answer the following.

1   The five virgins without oil in their lamps were called foolish. Why?

    _____

    _____

2   What foolish things do people do today that are like the virgins without oil?

    _____

    _____

3   How do you think a wise person prepares for the coming of Jesus?

    _____

    _____

1   Second letter of what Jesus compared His kingdom to in Mt 13:33
2   First letter of the reapers at the end of the world (Mt 13:39)
3   Fourth letter of the smallest seed of all (Mt 13:32)
4   Third letter of the stories Jesus told (Mt 13:3)
5   Second letter of the one who plants weeds among the wheat (Mt 13:25)
6   Last letter of the sower's enemy (Mt 13:39)
7   Second letter of the creatures who ate the seed on the footpath (Mt 13:4)
8   First letter of the place where the buried treasure was (Mt 13:44)

REMEMBER

How do we come to know the teachings of Jesus?
We come to know the teachings of Jesus through Scripture, Tradition, and the teaching of the Church.

What do we mean when we say Jesus taught in parables?
We mean that Jesus used stories of familiar things from the experiences of life to teach the people His doctrine.

RESPOND

Think about the unique way God wants you to contribute to the growth of His Church. Record it in your journal and tell how your example could influence others for the better.

Like Yeast in Dough

True Christians are like yeast or leaven in dough. What they say and do influences others. Listed below are several situations that present a dilemma to youth who want to follow Christ. A Christian response could easily entail ridicule or rejection by others.

Read each situation. List the decision you think a person guided by Christ's truth should make. Then list a way a person who did that could be ridiculed or rejected. Finally, decide what your decision would be in view of the possible reaction. Be ready to share your answers with the class.

1   Your friends start teasing an unpopular classmate who is trying to make friends.

Christian Response   Possible Reaction

_____   _____

Final Decision_____

2   Someone hands you pornographic pictures at school.

Christian Response   Possible Reaction

_____   _____

Final Decision_____

3   You're out with some friends. They decide to hitchhike just for the fun of it. Your parents have forbidden you to ride with anyone you don't know.

Christian Response   Possible Reaction

_____   _____

Final Decision_____

4   You and several others are at a friend's home. Your friend's parents are not there. The friend suggests drinking some of their liquor; there's a lot of it and the parents won't miss it.

Christian Response   Possible Reaction

_____   _____

Final Decision_____

5   A classmate you'd like to be friends with has dared you to do something dangerous. You realize you could seriously injure yourself if you try it and don't succeed.

Christian Response   Possible Reaction

_____   _____

Final Decision_____

I have come so that they may have life and have it to the full.

John 10:10

A New Way of Thinking

Challenges. This word alone inspires some people to do their best, try their hardest, give their all. Some people, on the other hand, are afraid of challenges.
What about you?

When you are given a project in school, how do you react?

When your friends want to lie to their parents about their plans for the weekend or about trouble they were in, how do you react?

Your reactions to daily challenges in life tell people a lot about you. Your actions show much about your attitudes and beliefs.

SERMON ON THE MOUNT

Jesus demands of us an entirely new way of thinking. When He spoke to the crowds, some of the people became angry. Others listened for a while but then turned away. And there were some who listened and accepted the new way of thinking.

What did Jesus say that was so completely different? What challenged those who heard Him? What did He teach that captivated the hearts of some and angered others?

In the Sermon on the Mount in the Gospel of Matthew (Matthew 5-7), you can find a collection of some of the teachings and sayings of Jesus. There Jesus climbs a hillside and gives the people a new understanding of the law, just as Moses once climbed Sinai to receive the law. The new law Jesus came to reveal was God's vision of the law. No longer were people simply to follow a set of rules. They were to be followers of a Person, followers of Jesus. Here Jesus taught them the type of life expected of those called to His kingdom.

10

BUT I SAY . . .

Jesus gave six examples of how the law was to be lived. Read the Scripture references listed. On the lines provided, write the fuller meaning Jesus brought to the law.

Matthew	You have learned how it was said . . .	But I say . . .
5:21-26	You must not kill.	_____ _____
5:27-30	You must not commit adultery.	_____ _____
5:31-32	Divorce was permitted.	_____ _____
5:33-27	You must not break an oath.	_____ _____
5:38-42	An eye for an eye, a tooth for a tooth.	_____ _____
5:43-48	Hate your enemy.	_____ _____

Check the statements that summarize what Jesus was saying:

1 ____ You must have love inside.
2 ____ You must do more than externally obey the law.
3 ____ God wants us to care for others, including our enemies and those who hurt us.
4 ____ The Old Law stated a minimum: at least do this much. But you are called to the maximum: there is so much more that you can and should do.

THE SPIRIT SETS YOU FREE

The law was God's will for His people, especially as expressed in the Commandments. Jesus did not come to destroy this law. But He indicated that something had been missing. The people were not living it as fully as God intended it to be lived.

They thought it was enough to obey the *letter* of the law: what they MUST do or what they CANNOT do. But they had missed the *spirit* of the law. The spirit goes much further. It sees beyond the duties listed in a law to the deeper meaning—to what the law was really calling them to be and do.

No longer would it be enough just to obey the letter of the law. Jesus stressed that a deeper understanding of the law was called for. A person needs to be aware of the law's inner spirit.

No longer would it be enough to do only what appeared to be right or good on the outside. The minds of the people needed to be filled with the truth and their hearts with love. Your motives—the reasons behind your actions—are important.

To serve the Lord in spirit and in truth is the way to the kingdom. By the truth, you know what God wills and what can bring you real happiness. By the spirit, you are enabled to do what God wants of you. You are able to love God without limit and love others as Jesus has loved you. This was the new way of thinking and living Jesus revealed.

LIFE AND VALUES

You, too, are called to a new and deeper understanding of law. Good laws have meaning and protect certain values. As you grow, you begin to see more and more of these reasons and values.

- Laws protect freedom, values, and the rights people hold as important.
- Laws protect the common good.
- Laws help people reach goals and live with dignity.

When you are able to see the value behind a law, you are able to live in the spirit of that law.

> Four or five years ago, how did you understand the meaning of the rule: Cross the street at the crosswalk?
>
> How is your understanding of this rule deeper now?

TWO SIDES TO A LAW

Laws may be expressed in two ways. They are *negative* when they express what you may not or should not do. They set definite limits. They are *positive* when they command an action you should or must do.

Jesus expressed law in both positive and negative ways.

> Read Matthew 22:37-39. Is this a positive or negative law?
>
> _____
>
> Read Matthew 7:1. Is this law expressed as a negative or a positive law?
>
> _____

On the lines below rewrite the Ten Commandments in a positive form, telling what you SHOULD do, and not only what you must NOT do.

1 _____

2 _____

3 _____

4 _____

5 _____

6 _____

7 _____

8 _____

9 _____

10 _____

MORE THAN COMMANDS

Behind each commandment is a value—something to be reverenced, guarded, loved. Understanding the value behind the law will help you live in the spirit of that law.

The Law of Love

You shall not kill (Exodus 20:13). How simple that sounds. You must love your neighbor as yourself (Matthew 19:19). That, too, sounds so simple. But the law of love—and the spirit of love—really touches every part of your life. This law is not always so simple.

LIFE: A PRECIOUS GIFT

What makes your life important? Is it because you have certain skills or talents? Is it because you get good grades in school or work very hard? Is it because you may be healthy, athletic, or good-looking? Is it because your family is wealthy? Or because people listen to you and what you have to say?

None of these things makes your life—YOU—important. Your life is valuable because it comes from God. It is His gift and only He may give or take it. And life—your life and the lives of others—is not limited to this life on earth. This life is very important, but it leads to a greater life, life to the full, eternal life.

Jesus said you must do more than avoid taking life. What God wants is that you love and care for all life, especially for human life. He wants you to care not only for all human life on earth but also for the new life of the spirit which will reach the fullness of the kingdom.

You care for your physical life by taking reasonable care of your health. Proper eating and sleeping habits are important for growth and health. Much has been discovered about how junk food and the abuse of drugs, alcohol, and tobacco can harm you. It is your responsibility as a Christian to avoid all that could hurt you unnecessarily.

You care for your life of the spirit by being concerned about your spiritual growth. Your prayer life, the way you worship and try to live according to God's will are important. The good habits you try to make part of your life are signs that you know your friendship with God is important, too.

List three things you have done today that show you are taking reasonable care of your health.

_____

_____

_____

List three things you have done today that show you are concerned about your spiritual life and growth.

_____

_____

_____

THE MANY FACES OF LIFE

Love is an easy word to use, but it has some very big demands. Some of its demands touch your life right now. Many of them require sacrifice and courage.

SCANDAL

It's easy to see how fights can harm people. It's easy to see how unkind words can wound. But there is another way to hurt others that we sometimes forget. That way is by giving bad example and scandal.

You learn much from others. Although you can grow and be encouraged by seeing others do good things, you can also be harmed by seeing them do the opposite. This is true for all people, but especially for younger children. Children look up to older brothers and sisters and want to imitate them. They may not understand fully what makes an action right or wrong; they may simply follow.

Jesus was concerned about this problem of example. Read His words in Matthew 18:5-7 to find out how serious bad example can be.

But if giving scandal is so harmful, then giving good example is one of the most powerful ways we can teach others and bring them to Christ.

ABORTION

Some countries have made abortion legal under certain conditions. A law may make it legal, but it cannot make it right.

Abortion is the killing of the fetus, the developing baby, before birth. A baby has rights but cannot defend itself. Children with handicaps or deformities have a special claim on the protection of others. The gift of their life is precious. Every child denied life because of abortion has also been denied the right to know and love and serve God as a human being here on earth.

Without any doubt abortion is wrong. As a Christian you must do all in your power to prevent the killing of innocent children. You can pray that the Holy Spirit will enlighten people to see the value of all human life and the evil of abortion. You can help others appreciate human life by all you do to show respect and concern for the needs of people around you.

ANGER AND GRUDGES

Argue. Yell. Hurt someone's feelings. Chances are you have done some of these things. It may have been aimed at a parent, a friend, or your brother or sister. Most of these reactions come from being angry.

Anger is an emotion experienced by all. It comes more quickly to some. But few people really understand how anger can work for good or evil in their lives.

Anger that is out of control is bad and damaging. But anger can be good. It can supply the energy you need to change things you know are wrong. But it is very important to know how to channel this type of anger.

Jesus knew anger. He was angry with the money dealers in the temple (Matthew 21:12-16) and at those who were quick to judge others harshly (John 8:1-11). Jesus never lost control of His temper. His anger was motivated always by love: love of His Father, love for the people, love for us. He was always ready to forgive.

Did Jesus mock or make fun of others when He was angry?

Did He hold a grudge or ever refuse to forgive someone?

Did He physically harm any other person?

What type of things made Him angry?

Jesus was strong but He used His strength, even in anger, only to help others.

What two suggestions would you offer to a friend who has trouble controlling his or her anger?

1 _____

2 _____

SUICIDE

Sometimes life can seem too difficult or painful. Some people may feel it would be better to die than to go on with so many problems. Some turn to suicide as an answer to their problems. Suicide is the taking of one's own life deliberately. Suicide is seriously wrong.

Everyone has problems. Everyone feels pain at some time. Perhaps there are troubles in the family. Perhaps some persons feel they have failed at everything. Perhaps they feel unloved, friendless, and unlovable. Or they may feel they have done something so bad that they can never forgive themselves or expect anyone else to forgive them.

As you continue to grow, some of the difficulties you experience in life will seem worse at some times than at others. It is good to keep some basic ideas in mind when facing any crisis. Here are some suggestions:

1 Recall a problem from years past that you were able to solve. Remember how painful it may have been, but how you were able to handle it eventually. Things do change in your life with time. Be willing to give yourself that time.

2 Talk to someone who cares about what you are feeling and going through. It should be someone who can help in some way: a parent, teacher, counselor.

3 Try to become involved in activities, sports, or hobbies. Be with people who can support you.

4 Try to reach out to others who may be experiencing pain. Learning to care for others may take the weight from your problem.

5 Bring your concerns to God and ask for His help and guidance. Trust that His love for you is more than you can ever imagine.

16

EUTHANASIA

What value is there in illness or growing old? Some people do not know the answer to that question. Some fear pain. Some think they are important only if they can work or at least be physically active.

Euthanasia, or mercy-killing as it is often called, is the direct causing of death by painless means for the purpose of ending human suffering. Sometimes people defend it as a kinder way to treat those who suffer. But such a view is far from that of Christ. Jesus Himself knew pain and suffering. He reached out to those crippled and burdened with age.

How can we understand illness and aging from a Christian point of view? First of all, God alone creates. He alone has the right over your life and death. Secondly, illness and aging may help the Christian community in many ways. Seeing others in pain may call forth love and courage from you. This love is good. This care and concern for the sick or elderly is good. Thirdly, illness can prepare us and others for eternal life. It can help us realize that God is the most important One in life. Finally, sickness and aging are part of God's plan. There will be mystery in many things that happen to you and others. But you can trust that the God Who has gifted you with life will use all things for your good.

REACH OUT

1   What is the meaning of "It is not enough to be anti-abortion; you must also be pro-life"? Write your response. Then ask a parent, a grandparent, and an older teenager to comment on the same quote.

2   Read Psalm 136 or Psalm 148. Illustrate either one of the psalms or compose your own litany of thanksgiving or song of praise patterned after them.

3   Charity begins at home! Try one of these.
   • Go to bed on time for a week.
   • Lead an original prayer at home before a meal.
   • Give up using your allowance on yourself and use it in some way for your family.
   • Offer to do two extra jobs at home to replace the ordinary turn of someone else in your family.

REMEMBER

What is the main message of the Sermon on the Mount? Christ proclaimed a new way to the Father by which He expects His disciples to live a more perfect Christian life.

Why must life be preserved and respected? All life is a gift from God to be lived, preserved, and respected for His honor and glory. Human life is a special gift because we are destined to live forever in His kingdom.

RESPOND

God calls us to love as He loves. Read 1 Corinthians 13:4-7. In your journal rewrite the same passage, replacing the word "love" with your own name. List one way in which you will try to live what you have written. Ask Jesus to help you grow in love.

Celebrating Life

Leader: The Lord our God has gifted us with life. We are called to care for that gift of life in ourselves and others. Let us celebrate life!

SONG AND PROCESSION WITH BIBLES AND CANDLES

READINGS AND RESPONSES

Leader: God has given us life by creating us. Jesus has given us life by redeeming us. The Holy Spirit leads us to the fullness of life in the Father and the Son. Let us listen now as God calls us to choose life.

Reader 1:   A reading from the book of Deuteronomy 30:15-20.

Leader: Let us pray.

All: Let us choose life today and always. We know that those who follow You, Lord, will have the light of life.

SONG RESPONSE OR ALLELUIA

Leader: We know we have love for God if we show love to others. Let us listen to the Word of God calling us to show our love in practical ways.

Reader 2:   A reading from the Gospel of Luke 6:27-38.

Leader: Let us pray.

All: We are Your people, Lord, called to love as You loved.

PRESENTATION OF SYMBOLS

Leader: We bring these symbols, signs of our desire to follow Your Word, Lord. Bless them, and bless us as we journey toward You in all we do.

(Symbols are placed on a special table.)

LITANY OF LIFE

Reader 1:   Let us thank the Lord of life for His many gifts to us. Our response is: Jesus, thank You for life.

Reader 2:   Whenever I walk down a hall, run in a field, jump for joy, I am saying . . .

Reader 2:   Whenever I share in Eucharist, gather with friends and family to pray, I am saying . . .

Reader 1:   Whenver I watch a sunset, walk on a beach, enjoy a rainy afternoon, I am saying . . .

Reader 2:   Whenever I forgive someone who hurts me, I am saying . . .

Reader 1:   Whenever I lend my arm to support the aged, or reach out to help a child, I am saying . . .

Reader 2:   Whenever I make a friend, or choose to say a kind word about another person, or think of others first, I am saying . . .

Leader: For all the "others" in our life, for all who love us and for all who do not, let us pray,
Our Father . . .

SONG

Give
and there will be gifts for you:
a full measure, pressed down,
shaken together, and running over . . .
because the amount you measure out is
the amount you will be given back.

Luke 6:38

> Happy those who hunger and
> thirst for what is right:
> they shall be satisfied.
>
> *Matthew 5:6*

Those who "thirst for what is right" desire to keep their friendship with God. They seek to live according to the values Jesus taught and help others live this way. Can you risk doing what is right even though you know that other people will not accept you? Can you give up some of your money to help those in need? Can you use your time for others instead of yourself?

Look again at these questions. Write one thing you could do to live this Beatitude.

_____

_____

> Happy the merciful:
> they shall have mercy shown them.
>
> *Matthew 5:7*

Jesus is more interested in giving than in receiving. Look at His Life. He goes out of His way to forgive those who crucify Him. He is the first to be a friend to sinners, the first to love His enemies, the first to generously welcome the poor.

He expects us to imitate Him. Forgive! Serve! Treat everyone as a friend; the poor, the handicapped, the outcast. Give love without looking for any return.

Circle the one characteristic you need now to help yourself be merciful.

Courage	Forgiveness	Unselfishness
Patience	Generosity	Love

> Happy the pure in heart:
> They shall see God.
>
> *Matthew 5:8*

Study a wheel closely. Every spoke is attached to the center. Jesus' life could be compared to this. He did many things: curing, preaching, praying, discussing, and teaching. But the center, the heart of all His activity was His Father's will. Being "pure in heart" is to recognize Jesus in the center of your heart. It means that you let Jesus guide all the thoughts and decisions you make. Jesus wants you to have a single heart as He did. He wants you to use your gifts to do the Father's will.

Write down a time when you used your gifts to do God's will. How did you feel?

_____

_____

Happy the peacemakers:
They shall be called sons of God.

Matthew 5:9

Where does peace start? Jesus says in the heart. To be a peacemaker you must be at peace with yourself. You must accept your limitiations and your strengths. Then you can share your peace with others. Peace-making is contagious. It builds, encourages and strengthens the community. Jesus praises people whose peacemaking can lead others to become God's sons and daughters.

Check the statements that express true peace.

_____ Peace means everything goes the way you want.

_____ Peace means coming to grips with yourself — your strengths and weaknesses.

_____ Peace means not getting involved.

_____ Peace means going along with the crowd when there's trouble and praying you don't get caught.

_____ Peace means to forgive those who hurt you.

_____ Peace can mean conflict—that you will have to stand up for what is right.

_____ Peace means knowing that God made you and that you are valuable to Him and others.

Happy those who are persecuted in the cause of right: theirs is the kingdom of heaven.

Matthew 5:10

Sometimes people hurt you deeply by being unfair and ciriticizing you wrongly. Sometimes they can hurt you physically. If you are serious about living and helping others live the Gospel, you will find yourself persecuted. For Jesus this led to the cross. For us it may mean the same. As a Christian you are called to pick up your cross daily. You are happy to do this because it proves your personal love as a disciple of Jesus.

1   When someone speaks unkindly about you before school, you could show courage for the cause of right in speaking kindly to them during the day.

    Never   Sometimes   Always

2   When your brother or sister uses one of your things which they have no right to use, you could forgive them.

    Never   Sometimes   Always

3   When you have done something wrong, you should have the courage to admit it and take the consequences.

    Never   Sometimes   Always

4   When you disagree with your friends and refuse to go along with something because it is wrong, you are showing courage for the cause of right.

    Never   Sometimes   Always

Called to Be a Disciple

Is Jesus your friend? Can you be His follower? That's what a disciple is—a friend and a follower. To follow Jesus you must first know Him. Do you really know Him? His highest ideals? His dreams? His deepest loneliness? The heroic deeds He did for love of us?

Do you really follow Jesus? He shows the way. It is the way of the Beatitudes.

DON'T COUNT THE COST

Jairus was a man whose twelve-year-old daughter was dying. He begged Jesus to come right away. An official arrived and announced that the little girl was dead. Jesus took charge and told everyone that the little girl was not dead but sleeping. They laughed because they did not believe in the power of Jesus to bring people back from the dead. But Jesus did not let their mockery stop Him from using His power to restore life to the little girl. He went over, took her hand and she got up. Then Jesus asked them to get her something to eat.

Based on Luke 8:40-56

Which beatitude do you think of when you see Jesus do good even when people laught at Him? Write it below.

GIVE COMFORT

Mary and Martha were upset. Their brother Lazarus was sick. By the time Jesus arrived, Lazarus was dead. Martha ran up to Jesus and told Him that if He had been there, her brother would not have died. When Mary and Martha took Jesus to the tomb, He wept. They all knew Jesus loved Lazarus very much. Then Jesus cried out in a loud voice, "Lazarus," and Lazarus walked out of the tomb.

Based on John 11:1-44

Which Beautitude do you think of as Jesus brought comfort to Mary and Martha?

BE GENEROUS

When rich people were putting their offerings into the treasury, Jesus saw them. He also noticed a poor widow putting in two small coins. He said that the widow was more generous than the rich people because she had given all she had.

Based on Luke 21:1-4

Which Beatitude asks you to give generously to the poor?

_____

_____

RISK IT!

The people asked Jesus for a sign to help them believe in Him. Jesus told them that if they ate the bread that He would give them they would live forever. The people thought these words were strange. Many stopped following Him. How disappointed Jesus must have been!

Based on John 6:51-70

Which Beatitude tells you that you have to suffer for doing what is right?

_____

_____

BE CALM

Jesus appeared to the disciples soon after the Resurrection. He knew they were afraid of being discovered by the Roman authorities. He knew they doubted whether they could teach His truth. He knew they could not even admit they were His friends. So Jesus says to them, "Peace be with you." Jesus showed that He had forgiven them and wanted to share His peace with them.

Based on Luke 24:36-43

Which Beatitude teaches us to extend our peace to others as Jesus did?

_____

_____

DEFEND WHAT IS RIGHT

When Jesus went to the temple, He saw people buying and selling there. He upset the tables of the money changers and the chairs of those selling pigeons. He risked the criticism of the temple dealers to protect the honor of God's house.

Matthew 21:12-13

Which Beatitude leads you to make decisions to defend what is right even if it means you must suffer the insults of others?

_____

_____

SEEK ONE GOAL

Once the Jewish authorities questioned Jesus about His right to cure the lame man on the Sabbath. Jesus explained to them that He did only the things the Father wants. He was sent by the Father and He came to do the Father's will.

Based on John 5:19-30

Which Beatitude do you think of when you hear that Jesus does His Father's will even when He must suffer the misunderstandings of others?

_____

_____

FORGIVE

Jesus was arrested and taken to the high priest's palace to be tried. Peter followed closely. A maid on duty at the door asked Peter if he was one of Jesus' disciples. Peter denied it. Peter loved Jesus but he was afraid to stand up for Him. Jesus forgave Peter because Peter was sorry.

Based on John 18:12-27

Even if people have hurt you unfairly which Beatitude says you should still forgive?

_____

_____

REVOLUTIONARY TEACHINGS!

That's what some people said about the teachings of Jesus. He said things that made people take a second look at themselves and their lives.

Read the teachings given below and circle the letters of those that are teachings of Jesus.

1 About Enemies
   a God will bring justice to those who hurt you.
   b Love of enemies is the sign of the true disciple.
   c You can't win so you might as well give in.

2 About Disciples
   a It is not hard to be a disciple of Jesus.
   b In order to follow Jesus you must discipline yourself.
   c There is very little joy in the life of a follower of Jesus.

3 About Serving
   a Give to others only when they give something to you.
   b Give away all you own.
   c Be willing to help and serve generously whenever you get the chance.

4 About Forgiving
   a Make sure people prove they are sorry before you forgive them.
   b Forgive but don't forget.
   c Forgive totally and do not hold grudges.

5 About Prayer
   a When you pray, say "Our Father . . ."
   b Only pray to God when things are hard for you.
   c There is no need to pray for God will do it all.

THE VALUES OF THE KINGDOM

Jesus tells you that when your values are in order, you will be happy. The Beatitudes challenge you to become a disciple of Christ. This is not easy because when you actively live the Beatitudes, your values will come in conflict with the world's. You will have to make choices.

Some people in the world say:
Get even!
Take as much as you can!
Settle for the easy way out!
Who cares about sharing!
What makes you feel good is the only thing that counts!

But the values of Christ's kingdom are very different.

Check all the statements that show the values of the kingdom according to the Beatitudes.

____ Forgiving makes you a stronger person.
____ Sharing is more freeing than selfishness.
____ Welcome people who are different than you.
____ Be sensitive to other people's pain.
____ Being honest builds trust.
____ Give away some of your possessions to help the poor.
____ Courage! Defend what you believe.
____ Stand up for people because you love them.

Me—a disciple? Yes, you!!! If you agreed to all the statements above, you already have the signs of becoming a disciple of Jesus.

REACH OUT

1 The Beatitudes tell us to look at our gifts and use them to help others. Think about how you can help out more at home. Decide on one new thing you can do. Talk to your parents about how you will carry this out. Or if you wish to make it a "hidden caring," write it in your journal. Check every day to see if you are keeping to it.

2 Read through Matthew 5 and 6. Pick out a favorite quote. Write it on paper, design it, and hang it in your room. It will be a reminder to share as Jesus did.

3 Kind words heal and help. Write a letter to one of your grandparents or someone who is sick. Share good news with them. This will cheer them up.

4 Look in your attic or your basement to see if you have extra clothes or shoes you do not use or need. Instead of throwing them away, ask your parents if you can give them away to those who may need them and can't afford them. Talk to your parents or teacher about where you can bring them.

5 Cut out of the newspaper articles that show people living the Beatitudes. Paste them on paper. Write out a summary of each story. Share them with your class or your family.

RESPOND

Do you want world peace? Then promote world forgiveness. St. Paul tells us the power of words in Ephesians 4:32. Look these words up. Think them over. Write in your journal about a time you spoke words of forgiveness. Tell how your words helped you and the other person.

REMEMBER

What are the Beatitudes?

The promises of happiness made by Christ to those who follow His teachings.

This is what Yahweh asks of you:
only this, to act justly,
to love tenderly
and to walk humbly with your God.

Micah 6:8

A Fair Deal

WHAT'S AT STAKE?

Do you ever find yourself feeling dissatisfied about what you have or don't have? Then you need to examine your values.

Rate on a 1-5 scale which is the most important to you. Number 1 = most important; number 5 = least important.

____ Money
____ Other people
____ Grades
____ Service to family and friends
____ Things you own (radio, clothes, etc.)

THE CALL OF ZACCHAEUS

Maybe you have found that you are putting too much value on things that don't matter. If so Jesus can help you, as He helped a man named Zacchaeus.

Read Luke 19:1-10 to find out how Jesus helped Zacchaeus put his values in the right place. Then circle the letters of all the correct answers in this exercise.

1 A title for this story could be:
   a Zacchaeus, the Sinner
   b It Pays to Be Short
   c A Change of Heart

2 Zacchaeus probably gave up his money because:
   a He knew he'd get caught
   b He knew Jesus saw his sincerity and freed him from his sins
   c Jesus threatened to punish him if he didn't change

3 When the people saw Jesus invite Zacchaeus to supper, they thought:
   a Zacchaeus did not deserve to have Jesus in his home
   b Zacchaeus bribed Jesus to come
   c Zacchaeus was going to get Jesus to become a tax collector too

4 The moral of the story is:
   a Be honest so you can be popular
   b Feeling guilty can make you honest
   c Jesus helps us be honest with God and others

5 We learn from Zacchaeus: (Choose as many right answers as possible.)
   a You are obliged to pay back to others what you have taken
   b Be willing to change your attitude
   c If you have made the mistake of being selfish, you can't change—so stay selfish
   d God does forgive
   e To follow Jesus means you can't have any money
   f None of these things happen nowadays

THE HEART OF THE MATTER

What did Jesus do about justice? There were plenty of poor in Jerusalem. The tax collectors, like Zacchaeus, robbed the poor and got away with it. Why didn't Jesus do something? Why didn't He raise an army, collect food and clothing?

He did do something! Jesus showed He was interested not only in changing things but in helping people grow and make decisions. This is what happened to Zacchaeus. He listened to Jesus, and that started him thinking. He faced up to the fact that he had robbed and cheated people. He saw that Christ loved him and was giving him a second chance. After Zacchaeus changed his attitude, he could change his actions. He gave one half of his goods to the poor. To those he cheated, he returned four times the amount he cheated them.

Jesus didn't force Zacchaeus and He won't force you. He helps you grow by loving you and forgiving you. When your values are the values of Jesus, you can be creative in discovering how you can use your talents to serve. The question is how do you start putting your values in order?

The seventh and tenth commandments help you put the right value on material things. The seventh commandment, "You shall not steal," tells you to be honest in what you do with your things and those of others. The tenth commandment, "You shall not covet your neighbor's goods," tells you to be honest and respectful in your attitude toward others and their things.

LOOK WHAT COUNTS

Persons are important. You are a very special person and more important than things. Here are some reasons. God created you to His image and likeness. He gave you unique talents and gifts with which to creatively improve yourself and to serve others. He has given you the right to possess property and to use it properly. He has done the same for every other person. That is why it is right to respect every person and his property. This is the spirit of the seventh and tenth commandments.

Look at your possessions. They can help you become a better person. They can help you grow in your friendship with God and with others. They can do the same for other people. But possessions must be respected and used as God intended. To do this you must protect your own property and the property of others. You must work honestly to earn things. You must look for ways to share what you have.

ENVY KILLS

Envy is feeling deprived or saddened over some material thing another person has or some success they've achieved. Envy kills any relationship with people. It means you love others so little, you will hurt people who have what you lack or achieve what you have not done.

When you are envious, you cannot appreciate people. An unhealthy competition grows. Sometimes competition is good because it keeps you from getting lazy. But unhealthy competition means you waste your time looking for the faults of others, comparing their talents to yours, and putting them down so you can get ahead. When you see these signs of envy in yourself, remember:

- God loves you for you are His.
- Ask Jesus to help you see the gifts God has given the person you envy.
- Make the decision to do something that will show you appreciate the goodness of that person.

1 What could teenagers want that would lead them to envy someone else?

_____

_____

2 Name something specific you can do to make another person feel important.

_____

_____

_____

GREED DESTROYS

Greed is the desire to possess and control things. It is the root of most wars. When people are greedy, they are no longer interested in protecting property. They want more than their neighbor. This may mean more popularity! More power! More attention! The desire is so strong, they are willing to spend all their time and energy getting it, even unfairly. Stealing and cheating come easily, but there is no lasting satisfaction in them.

People who steal and cheat do not respect the rights of others. When people's possessions are taken or their rights are not respected, they cannot become the best persons possible. They begin to lose trust in their neighbors.

Restitution is essential if you are to be forgiven by God and others for stealing, vandalism or any other offense against the seventh and tenth commandments. Restitution means to repair the damage caused. It can be done in several ways. If you steal, you must return the stolen item or pay for it. If you have damaged the stolen item or any item seriously and deliberately, you must pay for the damage. You may do this anonymously.

If you are having trouble being honest:

- Respect the property of others.
- Ask Jesus to help you make generous decisions about sharing your things.
- Make a decision to look for ways to care for the things you own in a responsible manner.

OPEN UP!

1 Do you think cheating on a test is as wrong as stealing from a store? Explain.

_____

_____

_____

2 What responsibility do you have when you borrow something?

_____

_____

3 What do you own now that you could share with others? Explain.

_____

_____

_____

4 How does it help other people when we do not waste food or material things?

_____

_____

_____

The Power of Words

Followers of Christ are people who value the truth. They speak the truth to one another and about one another. The truth helps them grow in Christian love. What do you know about telling the truth?

TAKE A SURVEY!

Find out what you know about telling the truth. Check *yes* or *no* to these statements.

		Yes	No
1	It's all right to lie if you don't get caught.	___	___
2	Most commercials on TV tell the truth.	___	___
3	If you love and accept yourself as a friend of God, you will tell the truth.	___	___
4	Adults always tell the truth.	___	___
5	When you lie, it hurts all of society.	___	___
6	You can remain silent about the truth to prevent injustice.	___	___
7	To tell the truth means to say anything that comes to one's mind.	___	___
8	A lie hurts only the one who tells it.	___	___
9	The people you can really trust are the ones who tell the truth.	___	___
10	It is all right to cover up to keep another out of trouble.	___	___
11	Rumors can be lies.	___	___
12	To tell the truth means to tell people honestly all of their faults.	___	___

VALUE THE TRUTH

Jesus knew the value of truth. He called Himself the Truth. Every action, every word He spoke showed a truthful way of living. He insisted that what we are in our hearts must be what God expects of us. Then what people see in our daily living will be the real truth. This way we communicate not only truth but personal love of people. We follow Jesus Who said, "Say 'yes,' when you mean yes, 'no' when you mean no; anything more than this comes from the evil one" Matthew 5:37. But our first "yes" must be to God, conforming our will to His divine will.

The truth is simple. It builds up relationships between you and other people. You need to know what others are thinking and they need to know what you are thinking. When people are truthful, they can love and trust each other.

Lying is destructive. It blocks out the truth and breaks down trust in ourselves, in others, and in society. God gave us minds to know the truth and hearts to go out to others in love. That is why He gave us the eighth commandment, which forbids untrue words and acts.

WHY DO PEOPLE LIE?

Fear is number one! Some people are afraid others won't like them. So they cover up and exaggerate. Being a phony isn't half as hard as being real. If you are a phony you don't have to admit, "I'm wrong," "I'm sorry," "I don't know."

To be on top is another reason. Some people want to impress others and get their attention. They may lie to win, to be popular, to get good grades, or to get out of work or trouble. But a lie only works for the moment. In the end a person loses friends, peace, and even friendship with God.

JILL'S CAMPAIGN

"Look who's running for student council!" remarked Marianne sarcastically as she looked across the hall. There stood Jill Woodchuster handing out campaign buttons to an excited crowd.

"Looks decent," said Matt to Marianne as he looked up from the homework he was doing.

"Shows what you know," answered Marianne. "She really thinks she's something."

"Well, she was class treasurer last year," Carol reminded the group around Marianne. "She was captain of the cheerleaders."

"Kids like her," claimed Bob.

"The teachers like her!" corrected Marianne smartly. "She's so sweet to their faces. The kids don't know about her or they wouldn't vote for her."

"The kids don't know what?" asked Carol curiously.

Marianne lowered her voice, "Well I'm only going to tell you. I heard that she took money from the class treasury last year and that she lifts stuff from stores when she needs it."

"I've never heard that," said Matt. "I wonder if it's true."

"I don't believe it," snapped Bob.

"You vote for her if you want. But I'm not," said Marianne firmly.

Carol turned around, "I didn't know she was *that* kind of person."

1 Do you think Jill really shoplifted and stole money?

2 What does Bob think of Jill?

3 What happened to Carol's opinion of Jill?

4 How has Marianne hurt Jill?

5 Do you think Marianne lied? Explain.

6 What do you think will happen because of this rumor?

WHAT ABOUT SILENCE?

Must you tell everything you know? Silence is necessary when you are tempted to spread gossip. It is needed to keep family secrets within the family and to guard other confidences.

You are already aware that priests, doctors, lawyers, secretaries and other professional people keep information about their work private in order to protect people's reputations.

BE TRUTHFUL

It will be easier to be truthful when you realize the great love Jesus has for you. Then you will try to love others as He did. His love will give you courage, and you will not be afraid to be truthful. It will help you to be unselfish and to think of others as well as yourself. Once you understand God's great love, you will begin to love more openly and truthfully.

WHAT DO YOU GET OUT OF BEING A TRUTHFUL PERSON?

You get a great deal. So does everyone else. Here are three benefits.

1 You get *courage* to be yourself. People can trust you and depend upon you. Their confidence gives you a certain freedom and peace that helps you be yourself.

2 You get *strength of character.* Truth builds character. You are in touch with God and what He can help you become. The decisions you make reflect the values of Christ. Instead of trying to get out of things, you are willing to take responsibility and cope with consequences.

3 You build up *trust.* True friendships are possible only when people are honest. When someone tells you a secret, it is their way of saying, "I trust you. I like you. I respect you." You would do wrong to spread that secret around. Trust is a way of respecting others. That is why you don't read another person's mail, letters, notes, diary, or journal unless they offer to share these with you.

When you build trust by being honest, you are building a better society. Society includes the people in your school, on the bus, in your neighborhood, and in your family. You are sharing Christ's love with others. You are creating His peace all around you.

HAVING PROBLEMS BEING TRUTHFUL?

Here's help! Make these rules your own.

1 PRAY — Confide in Christ your desire to be truthful. Ask Him to help you. Do this every morning.

2 THINK — Look at your real self. Christ loves you. He died to help you come to share eternal life with Him.

3 CHECK UP — Catch yourself exaggerating? Lying? Spreading rumors? Stop doing it.

4 SHARE — Look for the good in other people and share with them. It will help you know yourself better.

RESPOND

Read slowly John 14:23-27. What is the peace Jesus gives? It is not the peace that is free from troubles or difficulties. It is not an escape from reality. No, His peace is profoundly deep and permanent. It means being true in word and action.

Write in your journal an experience you had recently in trying to be truthful. Was it hard for you? What did you ask Jesus to do for you? How did He help you handle it?

REMEMBER

What do the seventh and tenth commandments tell us?

The seventh and tenth commandments tell us to be honest and to respect the property of others.

What does the eighth commandment tell us?

The eighth commandment tells us to be truthful in our words.

REACH OUT

1 Phone calls can be caring power. Call up some relative of yours and take the time to talk about his or her interests.

2 Compliments are caring power too. See how many times during a day you can give a compliment to members of your family or your classmates.

3 Make up a short one-act play. Tell about someone who stole something and show how he or she made restitution.

4 Remember that everything we use is property to be respected. Be careful with the things you have and use. See how well you can take care of them. Try cleaning your room and keeping it neat for one week.

5 Write an article for your school newspaper on the value of honesty as opposed to stealing or cheating. Tell how honesty makes the whole school better.

Do not let your love be a pretense;
. . . have a profound respect for
each other.

Romans 12:9-10

What Is Love?

LOVE OF FRIENDSHIP

"Sally's mom calls us twins because we are always together: talking on the phone, doing homework, going shopping. Sally is always there to help when I forget my lunch or run out of notebook paper. She seems to know when to tell a joke to cheer me up and when to leave me alone. With Sally I can be myself. I can say how I feel about things, ask her advice, give her ideas. We make all our plans together. And I know she feels the same way about me.

So I couldn't understand why she wouldn't try out for the school play with me. I thought she might be mad when I got the part, but she was really excited. She even made my costume and helped sell tickets. I'm so glad that we're friends!"

Find an example from the story to match each of these qualities of friendship.

Sharing time _____

Trusting_____

Respecting differences _____

_____

Helping_____

Valuing each other_____

_____

Friendship is one of the greatest gifts you can give to another person. In sharing your time, your affection, your personal thoughts and feelings, you are sharing a part of yourself. If your friend treats you in the same way, this is called mutual friendship.

Jesus had special friends, like Lazarus and Martha and Mary. He offered His friendship to the apostles and He still offers it to us today. But Jesus also showed a love which was greater than ordinary friendship.

GOD'S LOVE

The love which Jesus commanded His followers to have for each other is called *agape* love. It is a totally selfless love which leads us to do good for one another.

How does agape love differ from ordinary friendship? With agape love, I will love you as you are even if you do not return my love. I will do all I can to make you truly happy. The best example of this love is Jesus dying on the cross, because He gave Himself not only for those who would love and follow Him, but also for those who would reject or ignore Him.

For a description of agape love, read 1 Corinthians 13:1-8. Then read the following examples and put an A in front of the examples of agape love and an M in front of the examples of mutual friendship.

_____ 1 Of course you can have my extra pen. You loaned me one last Friday, Miguel.

_____ 2 So what if everyone is ignoring Greg? That won't stop me from eating lunch with him.

_____ 3 Even though she has hurt my feelings, I'll still be her friend.

_____ 4 I'm telling this to you alone, Marti, because we're friends.

LOVE IN MARRIAGE

"God created man in the image of himself . . . male and female he created them"
Genesis 1:27.

God has placed within each man and woman an attraction for each other. He wanted them to need and to enjoy each other. He wanted them to grow in friendship. But more than friendship, He wanted

a man and a woman
to join in a love
so deep,
so selfless,
that their two lives would blend into one
like two streams blending into one river.

This union made sacred by a marriage vow would last throughout life.

Read Ephesians 5:25-33 and complete the following comparison.

The love of marriage can be compared to

the love of _____

_____

When God calls a Christian man and a woman to make a lifelong agreement in marriage, He blesses their union through the Sacrament of Matrimony. Throughout their lives together, the couple will rely on the strengthening grace of this sacrament for help in difficulties.

The married love they will share includes both mutual friendship and agape love. Married love includes

- accepting and cherishing the children God sends them
- sharing all things
- treasuring the other person as he or she is
- being faithful until death
- meeting the joys and pain of daily life together

Circle the three qualities which you think are most needed by husbands and wives who want to deepen their love for each other.

honest	faithful	broadminded
gentle	forgiving	cheerful
fair	respectful	responsible

Married couples use their good qualities to grow in love and to build a good marriage. According to God's plan, they use the sacred gift of sex to express and deepen their love for each other, to create new life, and to form a family.

A GIFT FROM GOD

God has given each human person special powers and gifts which are sacred and holy. Among these gifts is one that is life-giving. This is the gift of sex, a power to bring human life into the world. In this gift God has given us a share in His own power to create life. God, by His own free will, calls life into being. Through the power of sex, God has permitted man and woman to cooperate with Him freely in this act of creation. It is so sacred that God intended that it be protected by the unbreakable bond of marriage. For those who are called to marriage, it is a sacred enjoyment that God has given along with the many responsibilities of raising a family. Some people—priests, sisters, brothers—are called to sacrifice this enjoyment for the love of God and for His kingdom.

Along with this gift of sex, God has given men and women a strong attraction for each other. As a young person matures, this attraction grows. When it is accompanied by mutual love between a man and a woman, it leads first to friendship, then to dating, and finally to marriage.

One reason God made the gift of sex so attractive is to help married couples express their love for each other and to encourage them to cooperate with Him in creating new life. Each new person is a new creation, a new hope for the world, and needs to belong to a loving family.

FAMILY LOVE

In families, there are many opportunities to share mutual friendship and agape love. When members are trying to love unselfishly, all should feel respected, cherished, and at home. Everyone is responsible for helping to build a loving family relationship.

Rank the following qualities according to their importance in building a loving family relationship. Number 1 is most important. Number 5 is least important.

____ interest in each member

____ honesty

____ money

____ patience

____ sharing time and activities

____ open communication

Jesus understands the love which family members have for each other because He was part of a family and because He is God. He is also aware of the difficulties which they face. Families, like people, live and grow. Sometimes death or divorce can separate family members, causing a sense of loss and much pain. At these times, too, Jesus is loving each member and wants to help, to heal, to be a part of the family. He knows that the members must make a special effort to support each other.

Consider for a moment the contribution which you make to your family. Think of one thing you can do to help support the members of your family. Write it here.

MEETING THE CHALLENGE

Would you wear your new outfit to clean the basement?

Would you try to wash the family car with motor oil?

Of course not. You would ruin your outfit and waste the motor oil by not using these items for the purpose for which they were intended.

This same principle applies to the use of our sexual power. Our happiness in this life and in the life to come depends on using the gifts God has given us in the way He intended.

The gift of sex and of self is far more precious than any material object. It is a gift that must be treasured and saved for marriage. The only love which this gift can honestly express is the total surrender of two married people who will support each other, no matter what happens in the future.

A CHALLENGE

Each person faces the challenge of learning to control this sexual power which is strong enough to be called a drive. If a person does not control his or her sexual drive, that power will begin to control the person.

What does this mean? Here is a comparison. Imagine you are riding your bicycle down a steep hill in the city. Gradually you are picking up speed. Trees and houses seem to be whizzing by. Then—the brakes don't work! You can't stop! The bike is taking you right into heavy traffic. What do you think will happen?

Write your reply below.

_____

_____

_____

The outcome of the story could be tragedy or relief. It all depends on a key question: who is in control? You will want to be in control of your thoughts, words, actions, your human powers. God teaches you what to do and gives you the power to do it.

A DOUBLE SAFEGUARD

God gave us two commandments to safeguard the sacred gift of sex.

Write the sixth commandment.

_____

_____

Write the ninth commandment.

_____

_____

In the sixth commandment God forbids any sexual act that is contrary to the sacredness of marriage. Any violation of God's plan for the use of sex, either alone or with someone else, is forbidden by this commandment.

In His plan God wants us to respect the gift of sex, not only in our words and actions, but also in our thoughts and desires. He tells us this in the ninth commandment.

CALLED TO BE CHASTE

These commandments also tell us to make positive efforts to practice the virtue of chastity. This virtue is a habit by which we continuously show respect for the powers God gave to bring life into the world. A chaste person recognizes that God intended these powers to be used only in the married state by the two partners and according to His divine will.

All people, both inside and outside the married state, must practice the virtue of chastity. Married people practice it by being faithful to their married partner, and by accepting the children God wants them to have. Unmarried people exclude the use of the power completely.

Christ challenges us to become perfect as our heavenly Father is perfect. In order to become the persons He calls us to be, we must be chaste in our thoughts, words, and actions.

In Matthew 5:27 we read what Christ teaches. Write what He says.

_____

_____

_____

Paul, the apostle, taught the same message that Jesus taught about chastity. He explained why we should be chaste. Read 1 Corinthians 6:19, 20 and write the reasons Paul gives.

_____

_____

_____

BREAKING THROUGH ILLUSIONS
Which line is longer?

Have you ever been fooled by an optical illusion? A design can appear to be something that it isn't.

Illusions are not just found in designs, but also in false ideas and opinions. Whenever an idea appears appealing, but it is not actually according to God's plan, it offers an illusion of goodness. It is a trap.

DON'T BE FOOLED

In our world today, many people do not recognize the true value of the gift of sex. They act on illusions. Here are some. Can you explain why these are illusions?

- Using sexual powers can prove love and popularity.
- The gift of sex may be used for entertainment.
- Using language which makes fun of sex is adult behavior.

AN ACTION PLAN

One way to break through the illusions about the gift of sex is to develop the habit of chastity. In order to live a chaste life, Christians of all ages must follow an action plan.

WORD BOX

modesty   self-control   prayer to Mary   chaste

receiving Jesus in the Eucharist   loved by God   values

Read the plan and fill in the answers. Use the word box.

STEP ONE: DEPEND

DEPEND on God's power to enable you to practice chastity, to make right decisions and to be self-controlled according to God's will.

To the list below, add more helps to chastity.
- daily personal prayer
- reading the Word of God daily
- receiving frequent Holy Communion
- receiving the Sacrament of Reconciliation
- _____
- _____

STEP TWO: DECIDE

DECIDE to reverence yourself and all you have been given by God. You are valuable because you are

_____

STEP THREE: DISCIPLINE

DISCIPLINE yourself. Do not always choose the easy way in life. Strong, unselfish people always show

_____

STEP FOUR: DO

DO use common sense. If you take care that the books you read and the movies and television programs you watch are those that have a respectful attitude toward sex, it will help you to be

_____

It you dress, speak and act in a way which shows you respect yourself and others, you will be practicing

_____

STEP FIVE: DEVELOP

DEVELOP healthy friendships with young people who agree with your

_____

STEP SIX: DISCUSS

DISCUSS any problems or questions with a mature adult. Name one adult you may consult.

_____

REACH OUT

1 Fold and divide a piece of paper into six squares. At the top of each square, put a key word from the Plan of Action: DEPEND — DECIDE — DISCIPLINE — DO — DEVELOP — DISCUSS. Then read Ephesians 2-4. As you find an idea which will fit with one of the steps, copy it into that square.

2 Real friends challenge each other to be the best persons possible. Think of three ways that you can support your friends in chastity. List them in your journal.

3 If you are a girl, check the moral qualities which you most admire in boys your own age. If you are a boy, check the moral qualities you most admire in girls your own age. Discuss them at home with some members of your family explaining why each good quality appeals to you. Ask them to tell which qualities they most admire and why.

____ kindness	____ honesty
____ prayerfulness	____ truthfulness
____ gentleness	____ self-control
____ justice	____ friendliness
____ prudence	____ forgiveness
____ courage	____ unselfishness
____ respect	____ compassion

4 Choose a popular song that you think expresses true Christian love. Then ask yourself some questions on love as it is presented in the song.

Why is it like Christ's view of love?

How can it make you a better person if you live this song in practice? If you can't think of a song, ask someone in your family to help you.

REMEMBER

What is the purpose of the sixth and ninth commandments?

The purpose of the sixth and ninth commandments is to protect marriage and the sacred gift of sex.

In God's plan, when is the gift of sex to be used?

In God's plan, the use of the gift of sex is reserved for marriage.

RESPOND

Jesus understands the changes you are going through. He sees you growing and learning to deal with the many ups and downs of life. He understands your efforts and wants to offer you His help. In your journal, write a personal note to Jesus asking Him for help with a difficult situation or a person who may be troubling you. Thank Him for the help He has already given.

Choose a step in the Action Plan which will help you lead a chaste life. In your journal, list practical ways that will help you live that step.

Make your home in me, as I make mine in you.
As a branch cannot bear fruit all by itself,
but must remain part of the vine,
neither can you unless you remain in me.
I am the vine, you are the branches.

John 15:4-5

Gathered In My Name

THE NEW LAW OF LOVE

Some people spend a great deal of time hoping to discover heroic ways to help others. At the same time, many young people have found simple but powerful ways to serve. What secret lies behind their deeds?

Every day when Molly came home from school, she straightened up the house and began supper. Sometimes she even had time to start her homework before her mother returned from work. Molly's friends stayed around school or met together at other places just for fun. But Molly knew she couldn't afford the time to be with them always. Her mom depended on her, and even though no one knew how hard it was for her, she did it all because she loved her mom so much.

Jackson became involved in volunteer work at a nursing home as part of a class service project. He enjoyed the work most of the time, but there were some days when it was hard to be with people who were ill and suffering. Sometimes it was just difficult being faithful to the work. He had to give up a lot of his free time and even sacrifice some activities with his friends. But no matter how tired he was after work, he always felt better about life and about sharing.

When John celebrated his birthday, he received money from aunts, uncles, and even his older brother and sisters. He wanted to use it wisely, but he also wanted to spend some of it just for himself. So he put half of it into the bank. He could use it for gifts for the holidays. The rest would be his own. In class one day, his teacher had shown a film on the work of the missionaries. After it, the class was told that anyone who wished to make a contribution to the missions could. John thought about it a long time. Finally, he put the rest of his money in an envelope, sealed it, marked it ''mission money,'' and placed it on the teacher's desk. No one saw him do it; nor did he tell anyone of the sacrifice he had made.

List one or two reasons why Molly, Jackson, or John did what he or she did.

_____

_____

Which one of the three do *you* think showed the most love? Why?

_____

_____

Have you ever done anything like Molly, Jackson, or John did? If so, what was it? How did you feel about it after?

_____

_____

_____

_____

BRANCHES AND THE VINE

Young people all over the world are involved in serving others, sacrificing their time and money, because they have discovered the secret of the vine and branches.

What is the secret?

Look at any bush. If you break one of its branches, the leaves on it wither while the rest of the tree flourishes. One way you can tell the good branches is by seeing their fruit, growth, and beauty.

Your life as a Christian is very much like that healthy branch. If you are united to Christ, the true vine, it will show. It will show in how you treat others. It will show in how you look for ways to do things for others rather than wait for them to do things for you. This is the fruit you bear: your service to others, your love for them.

So people serve because they are united to Christ. To love Jesus means to love and serve others just as He loved and served them. Only by being united to Him can you find the strength to love.

People also serve because they wish to remain united to Christ. One way to remain united is to live as He lived.

In His Last Supper discourse, Jesus told His disciples many things. He gave them a new law: "Love one another, as I have loved you" (John 15:12). But He not only told them to love. He also showed them how to live this new law by giving them an example of service—service based on love.

Jesus did this by washing the feet of His disciples. He told them He would give His life for them and for us. He gave and He served, not because it felt good or pleased the people, but because He loved as His Father did. He loved selflessly. He loved consistently. He showed that the love He received from the Father and gave to us is a love that gives all, suffers all, and believes all. God's love for us is the secret, the power behind the service of a Christian—and it is yours through Jesus.

Remaining in Him requires service, selfless giving, and a warm hospitality that reaches out to all.

ALL SORTS OF WAYS

Perhaps you are not sure how God wants you to serve or reach out to others. How can you find out what you are called to do?

First, look at your life right now. Perhaps your service is to be like Molly's—serving the people right in your own family who need you. At home, at school, in your neighborhood, there are many simple meaningful ways to serve.

But is there more that you can do? Do you find that you have extra time with nothing really scheduled or planned? Perhaps in your life you can look for an additional type of serving. Like Jackson, you may be able to volunteer your time and talents at a nursing home, at your parish, by babysitting or by organizing projects for younger children.

Perhaps you do not have extra time. Or maybe you do not have many opportunities for service available in your area. But you are still able to contribute to the missions, to clothing and food drives, and to many other things.

No matter what your situation is, you can pray for those who are in need of the love, care, and help of others. All of us are called to this very important responsibility in life.

LIVING AS ONE

Part of "loving one another" means serving others. But another part of love is reaching out to others in warm hospitality. When Jesus said "Love one another," He told us He wanted His love to unite us in community.

_____

Write four things you like to do.

1 _____

2 _____

3 _____

4 _____

If you prefer to do the activities listed with other people, put a check (√) beside them. If you prefer to do them alone, mark an (x) beside them.

_____

Most people like to share their joys and their sorrows with others. You can feel at ease with people who share your beliefs, interests, and values. You can show your love by sharing yours with them.

Jesus understood our need for this kind of sharing. As Catholic Christians we do share beliefs and values. We are called to be one in Christ. We are called to form a Christian community. But there is more to community than just sharing activities or spending time together. Christian living is rooted in God's love, even though it can start with very simple things.

What was the very first community you belonged to?

_____

How can you build community? How can you help people experience warmth, love, and acceptance in Jesus Christ? Here are a few suggestions:

- welcoming a new student into class
- greeting people going to Church
- taking time to write a card to a friend or to a parishioner who is ill
- volunteering to do someone else's duties
- letting new members join the team, even if the season has begun already
- sharing supplies or lunches
- congratulating others on a success
- inviting others to join you in the cafeteria

Can you think of any others to include on the list?

_____

_____

_____

Empowered By Jesus

IT TAKES POWER

Power comes from various sources: water, the wind, the sun, oil. People continually seek out these sources for help—running their homes, farms, factories—you name it! There are so many needs and uses for power.

Consider a simple light bulb. It can transform a dark room into light in an instant. But it is of no use at all unless it is connected to some source of power. Once connected, it produces light, brightness, even warmth.

Your life and your desire for good is like that light bulb. You have many gifts, much potential. You can bring much brightness and happiness into the world and the lives of others. But where is the real source of your power? Where can you find the power to live the truth Jesus taught?

How can you be strong enough to love your enemies, sacrifice time and money for others, or go against the crowd to live according to Christian principles?

Your power is the power of Someone working within you. It is the power of the Holy Spirit, Who enables you to love as Jesus does.

Jesus knew it would not be easy for those who followed Him:

> In the world you will have trouble,
> but be brave:
> I have conquered the world.
>
> John 16:33

So He promised to remain with you in His Spirit. He is with you, too, in those around you who share your beliefs. And because you share His own life, you are filled with His power, His grace-life.

THE CARDINAL VIRTUES

At Baptism you received the Holy Spirit and many gifts that help you to love as Jesus does. Some of these powers are called the moral virtues. There are many moral virtues, but four of them are so important they are called the "cardinal" virtues. The word cardinal means "hinge." Just as a door works because of its hinges, so, too, your life is in good order when it is guided by these four special gifts.

The four cardinal virtues are prudence, temperance, justice, and fortitude.

PRUDENCE: DECIDING ON OUR ACTIONS

Prudence is the moral virtue that enables you to decide how to choose or how to prepare yourself for any situation. Prudent people ask other responsible people for advice. They think through their own beliefs and what they have learned. They try to discover what should be done and what should be avoided. After they have made a decision, they are willing to do what they must to stick by it.

TEMPERANCE: CONTROLLING OUR DESIRES

Temperance is the moral virtue that enables you to control your desire for pleasure. Temperance helps you curb tendencies to overdo it in eating, drinking, in the way you dress, act, and speak. Temperance leads you to think before you do things and to control your desires when necessary.

JUSTICE: GIVING OTHERS THEIR DUE

Justice is the moral virtue that enables you to respect the rights of others and give them their due. It gives you the determination to protect those rights and fulfill your responsibilities to them and to God.

FORTITUDE: COURAGE TO DO OR ENDURE

Fortitude is the moral virtue that gives you the courage to do what is right. But it is also the courage to resist doing foolish or reckless things. True Christian courage will require patience: the battle may be long and hard. The courage to follow Christ will require generosity: giving up something for someone else. It is the courage to resist sarcasm and ridicule from others at times, to overcome peer pressure.

REACH OUT

1 Think of someone you know who practices one of the moral virtues. Describe a particular instance when his or her behavior showed this virtue. Write it on good paper and, if possible, illustrate it.

2 Draw up a Family Community Guide to help your growth as a family. Together with the other members of your family, list all the things that help build community at home, those things that foster true love, the special customs and celebrations within your family, how you pray together, etc.

3 Rate yourself: How often do you go out of your way to help other people? How do you put your faith into practice? What are you doing in your home, your school, your neighborhood, to show you care?

4 Read John 13-14. Imagine you are there as Jesus is speaking. What would you think? What questions would you ask? Write these down.

REMEMBER

What are moral virtues?

Moral virtues are those gifts received at Baptism that have to do with conduct or behavior. The principle moral virtues are the cardinal virtues: prudence, fortitude, temperance, and justice.

RESPOND

Choose one of the moral virtues and write a prayer to the Holy Spirit asking for guidance in practicing that virtue. Write your prayer in your journal.

If we live by the truth and in love,
we shall grow in all ways into Christ.

Ephesians 4:15

HAPPY ATTITUDES

Another way to translate the word "blessed" in the Beatitudes is "how happy!"

How would you define happiness?

_____

_____

Who is the happiest person you know?

_____

What has this person said or done that makes you think he or she is so happy?

_____

_____

_____

Why was Jesus happy?

_____

_____

What could each of these people do to be happy?
Miguel wants to be poor in spirit:

_____

Andrea heard about peacemakers and wants to be one:

_____

Sean wants to be pure in heart:

_____

PARABLE PARTNERS

Which parable would help you solve each of these problems?

1 Envy or greed
2 Unforgiving
3 Selfish; uncaring
4 Careless about using your gifts

The Rich Man and Lazarus   Luke 16:19-31
The Good Employer   Matthew 20:1-16
The Unmerciful Servant   Matthew 18:23-35
The Talents   Matthew 25:14-30

HELP WANTED

How would you respond to the following letters? Write your answers on a separate sheet of paper.

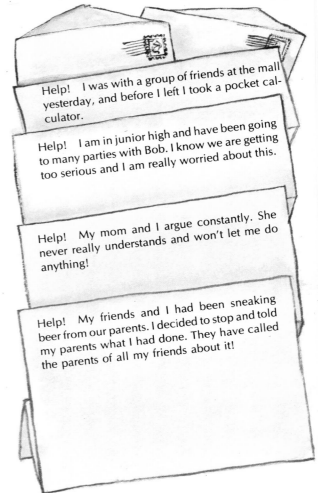

Help! I was with a group of friends at the mall yesterday, and before I left I took a pocket calculator.

Help! I am in junior high and have been going to many parties with Bob. I know we are getting too serious and I am really worried about this.

Help! My mom and I argue constantly. She never really understands and won't let me do anything!

Help! My friends and I had been sneaking beer from our parents. I decided to stop and told my parents what I had done. They have called the parents of all my friends about it!

NOW SWITCH! Choose one of the situations described above. Imagine yourself in the same situation.

What would you normally do in this kind of situation?

_____

_____

_____

How do you *wish* you could handle such situations?

_____

_____

_____

PUZZLING POSSIBILITIES

Fill in the crossword puzzle. Then unscramble the circled letters and put them in the box to find the special name given to the virtues of prudence, justice, fortitude and temperance.

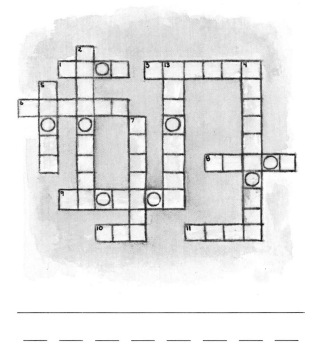

_____

__ __ __ __ __ __ __ __

_____

ACROSS

1,3 The One promised by Christ to be our strengthener; the One sent by the Father and the Son to live with us.

6 A power for or habit of doing good actions; the quality of living rightly.

8 Being or acting according to goodness; behaving according to standards of right conduct.

9 Help; as Jesus washed the feet of His disciples, He gave us an example of loving ____ .

10 United in everything important; Christ calls us to unity, to be ____ with Him and others. (See John 17:21.)

11 As branches we are to be united to Christ the ____ (See John 15:5.)

DOWN

2 Moral courage; the cardinal virtue by which a person does what is good and right in spite of difficulties.

4 The cardinal virtue by which one controls the desire for pleasure.

5 A part that enables a door, lid, etc., to open or turn; the meaning of the word "cardinal."

7 Fairness; the determination to give everyone what he or she has a right to.

13 Correct knowledge about what one ought to do and what should be avoided.

A TREASURE AWAITS THOSE WHO DARE

Christ has promised a treasure to those who follow Him. Discover what it is by filling in the missing vowels and separating the letters into words. To check your answer, search John 14. Is the treasure yours? Do you belong to Christ?

__ f__ n y__ n__ L__ v__ s

m__ h__ w__ l l k__ __ p m y

w__ r d __ n d m y F__ t h__ r

w__ l l L__ v__ h__ m__ n d

w__ s h__ l l c__ m__ t__ h__ m__

__ n d m__ k__ __ __ r h__ m__

w__ t h h__ m.

53

LOOKING BACK

In this book you have taken a look at some of the values and demands of Christian living. You have learned that Jesus calls you to live in His truth. He has called you as a member of the kingdom. Your attitudes, thoughts, and actions should show that you realize you are a member of that kingdom.

God asks you to base your decisions on His law and on the example of Jesus. He challenges you to respect life, to respect people and property, to live honestly, and to cherish the love within your family and the gift of sex. He empowers you with His Spirit and nourishes you in the Eucharist.

As you complete this unit, ask yourself three questions. Write your answers in your journal.

1 How has CHRIST JESUS, THE TRUTH helped me understand what Jesus asks of those who follow Him?
2 What will I try to remember when I am tempted or when others make it difficult for me to do the right thing?
3 What practical steps can I take to live the life of a disciple?

A PERSONAL INVENTORY

How well are you letting the principles Jesus taught guide your judgments and direct your actions? Circle a (always), s (sometimes), or n (never).

a s n   Do you think of what Jesus would want you to do or say in situations?

a s n   Do you go to people you respect for advice?

a s n   Do you see that little things in life (at home, at school) are opportunities to show respect for others and for property?

a s n   Do you ever go out of your way to serve others?

A PERSONAL REFLECTION

Below are some thoughts from St. Paul who tried to think and live according to the teachings of Jesus. Read them and spend some time thinking about them. Then think of situations in which you have shown love, faith, and a desire for purity. Write them on a paper.

Avoid anything in your everyday lives that would be unworthy of the gospel of Christ.

St. Paul (Philippians 1:27)

Do not let people disregard you because you are young, but be an example to all the believers in the way you speak and behave, and in your love, your faith, and your purity.

St. Paul (1 Timothy 4:12)

Stay with Us

JESUS REMAINS WITH US

Through His words and actions, Jesus taught us how to live the truth in love. But there is no way that we by our own efforts alone can follow His lead. He knew that.

He knew that we would need Him every step of the way—to teach us, to nourish us, to give us His power. Only with Him could we really love and obey our Father. Only with Him could we support and serve each other in unselfish love.

Knowing our need and wanting to stay with us, Jesus gave us the Holy Eucharist. In this sacrament, He is really present with us under the appearances of bread and wine.

In the Mass, or Eucharistic Celebration, Jesus continues to teach us by His Word and His example. He continues to offer His life for us and to nourish us with His Body and Blood. He unites us with Himself and with one another in the Christian community.

The reasons for participation in the Eucharistic Celebration are very important. We come to listen with open hearts to Jesus in the Liturgy of the Word. We come to be united with His tremendous love for the Father and for all His people.

THE LITURGY OF THE WORD

We listen as God speaks to us in the readings and as Christ proclaims His Gospel. We hear Jesus teach us what the Father wants us to know and what He wants us to do to lead a new life.

In the homily we listen as the priest or deacon helps us answer the question, "How does the Word of God in these readings apply to my life?"

THE LITURGY OF THE EUCHARIST

During the Liturgy of the Eucharist the sacrifice of Jesus on the cross and His resurrection become present to us. This total sacrifice of His life poured out for us gives us the light and strength we need to make the sacrifices God wants us to offer in our lives. We desire to bring our joys and hurts, our good acts and our failures—our whole lives—and offer them with Jesus to our Father. By this offering, we say, "Father, we belong to You."

List some life experiences which you can offer at the next Eucharistic Liturgy.

———————————————————————

———————————————————————

The Liturgy of the Eucharist is patterned after the Gospel account of Jesus' actions at the Last Supper. Read Luke 22:19-21 and write below what Jesus did with the bread.

———————————————————————

———————————————————————

———————————————————————

———————————————————————

HE TAKES BREAD

The Liturgy of the Eucharist begins with the Preparation of the Gifts. We take bread and wine to the priest at the altar. Then he says a prayer over each of these gifts. These prayers remind us that the bread and wine symbolize the gifts of God and the work of our hands.

What do we respond to each of these prayers?

———————————————————————

———————————————————————

HE GIVES THANKS

As the Liturgy of the Eucharist continues, the priest says a prayer of thanks called the Preface. With the priest, we offer thanks and praise with Jesus to the Father. We thank the Father for His Son Jesus Who became man and redeemed us through His cross and resurrection. Then we join the angels and the saints in a song of praise.

What is the first line of this song?

———————————————————————

HE OFFERS HIMSELF

The Preface leads into the Eucharistic Prayer, which is the high point of the entire act of worship. At this time the priest stretches his hands over the gifts and calls on the Holy Spirit to make these gifts holy. Jesus' Body and Blood become present on the altar under the forms of bread and wine.

The priest chooses one of four Eucharistic Prayers. At the Consecration, the priest uses words similar to those used by Jesus at the Last Supper.

Of the bread He said:

Take this, all of you, and eat it:
this is my body which will be given
up for you.

Of the cup of wine He said:

Take this, all of you, and drink
from it:
this is the cup of my blood,
the blood of the new and everlasting
covenant.
It will be shed for you and for all
so that sins may be forgiven.
Do this in memory of me.

From the Sacramentary

The presence of Jesus in the Eucharist and His offering to the Father is a truth that is so deep that we call it the "mystery of faith." At this time in the Mass, the priest invites us to proclaim this mystery. The Sacramentary gives us four possible memorial acclamations.

Write one of them here.

———————————————————————

———————————————————————

———————————————————————

We listen to the priest as he continues the Eucharistic Prayer. United with Jesus, we give praise to the Father. In union with Mary and all the saints, we pray for the Church on earth and for those who have died. The priest concludes this prayer with the hymn of praise:

Through him,
with him,
in him,
in the unity of the Holy Spirit,
all glory and honor is yours,
almighty Father,
for ever and ever.

From the Sacramentary

We respond by singing the great

HE GIVES HIMSELF

In the Communion Rite of the Mass, Jesus gives us His Body and Blood as food. We prepare for this by singing or praying together the prayer Jesus taught us, The Lord's Prayer.

As a eucharistic community, we exchange a sign of Christ's peace. We express our faith in the presence of the risen Christ who is the source of all peace. We are called to reconciliation and unity as we find and pray for peace for one another. As the priest breaks the bread, we pray that Jesus, the Lamb of God, will have mercy on us and grant us His peace.

Before receiving Jesus in Holy Communion, we say together a prayer that expresses both our weakness and our trust in God.

What is that prayer?

WE RECEIVE HIM

Our whole participation in the Eucharist is a preparation for Holy Communion. Nevertheless, we need to quietly focus our attention on His coming and tell Jesus of our desire to receive Him.

When we receive the Body and Blood of Jesus, He shares Himself with us and strengthens us. After the Communion song, each of us has time to converse with Him. We use this time to praise and thank Him and to tell Him of our needs. He will help us with all the problems we face. If we permit Him to act, He will gradually change us into the people He calls us to be.

As we all receive the Body and Blood of Jesus, we are drawn into union with the Father and the Holy Spirit and with each other. Here is a mystery. As we accept the Body of Christ in Communion, we also agree to accept and support one another in the Christian community.

HE GOES WITH US TO LOVE AND SERVE

Having been open to Jesus' love and transforming power, we become more aware of the needs of others and more able to serve them. With Jesus, we go forth to bring the Good News to all.

Some Things Every Catholic Should Know

THE TEN COMMANDMENTS

1 I am the Lord your God. You shall not have other gods besides Me.
2 You shall not take the name of the Lord, your God, in vain.
3 Remember to keep holy the Lord's day.
4 Honor your father and your mother.
5 You shall not kill.
6 You shall not commit adultery.
7 You shall not steal.
8 You shall not bear false witness against your neighbor.
9 You shall not covet your neighbor's wife.
10 You shall not covet anything that belongs to your neighbor.

PRECEPTS OF THE CHURCH

These are the duties that every Catholic Christian should follow.

1 To keep holy the day of the Lord's resurrection (Sunday). To worship God by participating in Mass every Sunday and holy day of obligation. To avoid those activities that would hinder renewal of body and soul.
2 To lead a sacramental life. To receive Holy Communion at every Eucharist and celebrate the Sacrament of Reconciliation regularly.
3 To study Catholic teaching in preparation for the Sacrament of Confirmation, to be confirmed, and then to continue to study and advance the cause of Christ.
4 To observe the marriage laws of the Church. To give religious training, by example and word, to one's children. To use parish schools and catechetical programs.
5 To strengthen and support the Church — one's own parish community and parish priests, the worldwide Church and the pope.
6 To do penance, including abstaining from meat and fasting from food on the appointed days.
7 To join in the missionary spirit and apostolate of the Church.

HOLY DAYS OF OBLIGATION IN THE UNITED STATES

SOLEMNITY OF MARY, MOTHER OF GOD: JANUARY 1.
We honor Mary, Mother of God.

ASCENSION: FORTIETH DAY AFTER EASTER.
On this day Jesus ascended into heaven.

ASSUMPTION: AUGUST 15.
We celebrate the fact that Mary was taken into heaven, body and soul.

ALL SAINTS' DAY: NOVEMBER 1.
We honor all the saints in heaven.

IMMACULATE CONCEPTION: DECEMBER 8.
We honor the fact that Mary was free from sin from the first moment of her life.

CHRISTMAS: DECEMBER 25.
We celebrate the birth of Jesus.

THE SEVEN SACRAMENTS

Baptism	Penance
Confirmation	Holy Orders
Holy Eucharist	Matrimony
Anointing of the Sick	

SPIRITUAL WORKS OF MERCY

Warn the sinner
Instruct the ignorant
Counsel the doubtful
Comfort the sorrowing
Bear wrongs patiently
Forgive all injuries
Pray for the living and the dead

THE CARDINAL VIRTUES

Prudence	Temperance
Justice	Fortitude

CORPORAL WORKS OF MERCY

Feed the hungry
Give drink to the thirsty
Clothe the naked
Visit the sick
Shelter the homeless
Visit the imprisoned
Bury the dead

THE BEATITUDES

Blessed are the poor in spirit;
  the reign of God is theirs.
Blessed are the sorrowing;
  they shall be consoled.
Blessed are the lowly;
  they shall inherit the land.
Blessed are they who hunger and
  thirst for holiness;
  they shall have their fill.
Blessed are they who show mercy;
  mercy shall be theirs.
Blessed are the single-hearted;
  they shall see God.
Blessed are the peacemakers;
  they shall be called sons of God.
Blessed are those persecuted for
  holiness' sake;
  the reign of God is theirs.

THE DIVINE PRAISES

Blessed be God.
Blessed be His holy name.
Blessed be Jesus Christ, true God
  and true man.
Blessed be the name of Jesus.
Blessed be His most Sacred Heart.
Blessed be His most Precious Blood.
Blessed be Jesus in the most Holy
  Sacrament of the Altar.
Blessed be the Holy Spirit,
  the Paraclete.
Blessed be the great Mother of God,
  Mary most holy.
Blessed be her holy and Immaculate
  Conception.
Blessed be her glorious Assumption.

Blessed be the name of Mary, Virgin
  and Mother.
Blessed be St. Joseph, her most
  chaste spouse.
Blessed be God in His angels and
  in His saints.

THE MYSTERIES OF THE ROSARY

JOYFUL MYSTERIES:
  The Annunciation
  The Visitation
  The Nativity
  The Presentation in the Temple
  The Finding of Jesus in the Temple

SORROWFUL MYSTERIES:
  The Agony in the Garden
  The Scourging at the Pillar
  The Crowning with Thorns
  The Carrying of the Cross
  The Crucifixion and Death of Jesus

GLORIOUS MYSTERIES:
  The Resurrection
  The Ascension
  The Descent of the Holy Spirit
  The Assumption of Mary
  The Crowning of Mary as Queen
    of Heaven and Earth

THE WAY OF THE CROSS

I   Jesus is condemned to death on
         the cross.
II   Jesus accepts His cross.
III   Jesus falls the first time.
IV   Jesus meets His sorrowful mother.
V   Simon of Cyrene helps Jesus carry
         His cross.
VI   Veronica wipes the face of Jesus.
VII   Jesus falls the second time.
VIII   Jesus meets and speaks to the
         women of Jerusalem.
IX   Jesus falls the third time.
X   Jesus is stripped of His garments.
XI   Jesus is nailed to the cross.
XII   Jesus dies on the cross.
XIII   Jesus is taken down from the cross
         and laid in His mother's arms.
XIV   Jesus is placed in the tomb.
XV   Jesus rises from the dead.

Glossary

abortion (uh BOR shun): The deliberate killing of the fetus, the developing baby, before birth. Direct abortion is seriously wrong.

adultery (uh DUL tur ee): the act of being sexually unfaithful to one's husband or wife.

agapé (ah GAPH pay): The love which Jesus commanded His followers to have for each other. It is a totally selfless love which leads us to do good for one another.

anger (ANG ur): An emotional sense of extreme displeasure.

Beatitudes (bee AT uh toods): The promises of happiness made by Christ to those who follow His teachings.

cardinal virtues (KARD un ul VUR chooz): The four main or "hinge" virtues which direct right living: prudence, justice, temperance, and fortitude.

charity (CHAIR uh tee): A virtue or power by which a person loves God above all things and loves all other people for God's sake.

chastity (CHAS tuh tee): A virtue or habit which helps us to control the desire for sexual pleasure according to God's law; the virtue of those who keep the sixth and ninth commandments.

covet (KUV it): To desire enviously what belongs to another; to want to take.

doctrine (DOK trin): Any truth taught by the Church that is to be believed; the teaching of the Church.

envy (EN vee): Sadness at another's success, talent, possessions, good fortune, etc. Envy is a sin against charity.

euthanasia (yoo thuh NAY juh): The act or practice of putting people to death because they or others decide it will avoid pain, or shorten suffering, or relieve others of the burden of caring for them. The word itself means "easy death."

fortitude (FOR tuh tood): Moral courage; the cardinal virtue by which a person does what is good and right in spite of difficulties faced.

greed (GREED): Too great a desire for wealth, possessions, power, etc.

justice (JUS tis): Fairness; the determination to give everyone what he or she deserves. Justice is one of the cardinal virtues which urges us to respect and protect the rights of all.

mercy-killing (MUR see KIL ing): another word for euthanasia.

modesty (MOD ihs tee): A virtue or habit which helps us to choose appropriate dress and behavior. It safeguards chastity.

moral virtues (MOR ul VUR chooz): Good habits of right living or behavior.

parable (PARE uh bul): A simple story that Jesus told to teach what God and the kingdom of God are like; a short story based on a familiar life experience used to teach a spiritual truth or a lesson of right living.

procreative (PRO kree ay tiv): Able to bring forth offspring or children; able to produce.

prudence (PROOD uns): Correct knowledge about what ought to be done and what should be avoided. Prudence is one of the cardinal virtues by which a person thinks before acting, makes wise choices, and follows through on decisions.

restitution (res tuh TOO shun): The act of repairing damage caused or returning to its rightful owner whatever had been unjustly taken from that person.

Sacramentary (SAK ruh MEN tu ree): The book which contains the prayers and directives for the celebrating of the Eucharistic Liturgy; part of the Roman Missal.

scandal (SKAN dul): Bad example that is likely to lead another person to sin. Scandal may be an act or an omission, refusal to act.

Sermon on the Mount (SUR mun ON THUH MOUNT): A collection of some of the sayings and teachings of the new covenant as recorded in the Gospel of Matthew, Chapters 5, 6, 7. The Sermon outlines the kind of life a true follower of Christ should live if he or she seeks the kingdom of God.

suicide (SOO uh side): The deliberate taking of one's own life.

temperance (TEM pur uns): The cardinal virtue by which one controls the desire for pleasure; moderation in eating, drinking, behavior, etc.

Tradition (truh DISH un): The message of Jesus which was handed on by the spoken words and example of the apostles and through the Catholic Church.